I0893955

Nos encantan las ciencias
So Into Science!

EXPLOREMOS EL CIELO DE NOCHE

EXPLORING THE NIGHT SKY

Emmett Martin
Traducido por / Translated by Eida de la Vega

Gareth Stevens
PUBLISHING

Please visit our website, www.garethstevens.com. For a free color catalog of all our high-quality books, call toll free 1-800-542-2595 or fax 1-877-542-2596.

Library of Congress Cataloging-in-Publication Data

Names: Martin, Emmett, author.
Title: Exploring the night sky = Exploremos el cielo de noche / Emmett Martin.
Description: New York : Gareth Stevens Publishing, [2019] | Series: So into science! = Nos encantan las ciencias | Includes index.
Identifiers: LCCN 2018013146| ISBN 9781538236284 (library bound)
Subjects: LCSH: Astronomy–Juvenile literature.
Classification: LCC QB46 .M37425 2019 | DDC 520–dc23
LC record available at https://lccn.loc.gov/2018013146

Published in 2019 by
Gareth Stevens Publishing
111 East 14th Street, Suite 349
New York, NY 10003

Copyright © 2019 Gareth Stevens Publishing

Translator: Eida de la Vega
Editor, English: Therese Shea
Designer: Sarah Liddell

Photo credits: Cover, p. 1 vovan/Shutterstock.com; p. 5 Pozdeyev Vitaly/Shutterstock.com; pp. 7, 24 (telescope) Celig/Shutterstock.com; pp. 9, 24 (constellation) danmitchell/DigitalVision Vectors/Getty Images; p. 11 alexkoral/Shutterstock.com; p. 13 TuiPhotoEngineer/Shutterstock.com; p. 15 David Carillet/Shutterstock.com; p. 17 Matej Pavlansky/Shutterstock.com; p. 19 Terrence Emerson/Shutterstock.com; p. 21 janez volmajer/Shutterstock.com; p. 23 Alohaflaminggo/Shutterstock.com.

All rights reserved. No part of this book may be reproduced in any form without permission in writing from the publisher, except by a reviewer.

Printed in the United States of America

CPSIA compliance information: Batch #CW19GS: For further information contact Gareth Stevens, New York, New York at 1-800-542-2595.

Contenido

Contents

Es de noche.
¡Veo muchas estrellas!

It's night.
I see so many stars!

Puedo ver más
con un telescopio.

••••••••••••••••••••••••••••••

I can see more
with a telescope!

Una constelación es
un grupo de estrellas.
Esta es la Osa Mayor.

....

A constellation is
a group of stars.
This one is
the Great Bear!

¡Veo una estrella fugaz!
No es una estrella.
Es polvo ardiendo.

••••••••••••••••••••••••••••••

I see a falling star!
It's not a star.
It's burning dust!

La Luna parece
un círculo.
Es luna llena.

....

The moon looks like
a circle.
It's a full moon!

La Luna a veces
se ve diferente.
A esto se le llama fases.

. . . .

The moon looks
different sometimes.
These are
called phases.

La Luna toma
la luz del sol.

....

The moon gets light
from the sun.

Puedo ver un planeta.
Es Venus.

....

I can see a planet.
It's Venus!

La Tierra da
una vuelta cada día.
¡Por eso tenemos
noche y día!

....

Earth spins around
each day.
That's why we have
night and day!

¡Me encanta
el cielo de noche!

• •

I love the night sky!